He Hates or GOD Hates
— Malachi 2:16 —

*The truth about
divorce, remarriage & singleness*

ANDY ECONOMIDES

DEDICATION

To Victoria and David.

You are a miracle for Jesus' Kingdom.

About the Cover, Ancient Hebrew Text

The cover for this book is an example of ancient Hebrew texts discovered at Qumran, Israel.

The Dead Sea Scrolls, also known as the Qumran Cave Scrolls, are ancient Jewish scrolls consisting of over 900 biblical and non-biblical manuscripts found in eleven caves at Qumran.

To find the true wording, and therefore meaning, of Malachi 2:16, this book considers ancient texts both Hebrew and otherwise. Included in the investigation we examine the Hebrew text from Qumran from manuscript 4QXII[a] which contains portions of Malachi 2:10 – 3:24.

Acknowledgements

A special big thank you to every friend and supporter of Soteria Trust who enable us to share the Good News of Christ Jesus in Britain and other countries. Thank you also to all those who today provide sponsorship to children, young people, and workers in Nigeria.

Thank you to Michael Mellows, the chairman and a trustee of Soteria Trust. You are a faithful and dear friend. Thank you to Robin Kemp, trustee of Soteria Trust. Robin has been with me from the start. Thank you for your loyalty and affection. Thank you to Martin Kitcatt, a former trustee of Soteria Trust, for many years of assistance to build a school in Africa. I miss you. I am very blessed with very talented and great staff at our Emsworth office with Roy, Lekan and Jana.

I would like to thank the beautiful children of God who supported and established the African mission school in Ibadan, Nigeria.

Thank you to: Revd Geoff and Jen Waggett, the friends at Christ Church in Ebbw Vale, Ian and Joanna, Peter and Wendy, Mike and Polly, Peter and Jennifer, Stuart Klein, Tim and Annette, Keith and Eileen, Chris and Cathy, David and Carolyn, Louise Stenhouse, and the friends of Tom Dodd.

I would also like to thank Robert Bennett for years of practical help at Soteria, David Elsey and John Sargent for praying every day, Gordon Braddock for your company and the fine guys in the Italian Men's Club. Thanks to Nicolino and the best Italian restaurant for raising support to educate needy children to attend the Soteria partner school in Nigeria, West Africa. I thank J.John and Killy for years of wonderful love and friendship.

REFLECTION

The church has been described too often as *'the army that shoots its own wounded'*. This book can help! As a close friend of the author, I know that he not only shares from his heart and his experience but always seeks to be faithful to his understanding of Scripture, to point out practical ways that we can and must do better in the areas of singleness, marriage, and divorce.

Andy Economides has written a punchy and readable resource here which challenges my own understanding and practice and took me back to the Bible again to work out these thorny issues that we all must reckon with. I will turn to *He Hates or God Hates* time and time again as I seek to help others, so that we can comfort others with the comfort we ourselves have received.

Revd Anthony Delaney
Ivy Church, Manchester
Author The B.E.S.T. Marriage

———————

Many people come to me in real dilemmas asking questions about their current emotional and stressful situations. They are hoping for greater insight and understanding from the Scriptures. One of the bigger biblical quandaries people struggle with, is the theology of marriage and divorce. Without deeper exploration, we can easily be polarised about what we think God is saying in some key theological areas such as marriage.

Andy Economides explores the area of marriage and divorce, researching the theological and contextual understanding of what God is saying about divorce in the Old Testament and what Jesus is saying about divorce in the New. The desire is to find out the truth of what God is really communicating in context and to understand what that means for those who struggle with this subject today.

Revd Tim Saiet
St John's Church, Tonbridge, Kent

———————

He Hates or God Hates ~ Malachi 2:16 is theologically sound and biblical, interesting, and down to earth. Andy Economides' book is extremely practical and very relevant for today's church. This book will be an asset to any pastor or minister of the gospel in the fresh perspectives it offers the Christian or practitioner.

Rt Revd Dr W. Karowei Dorgu
Bishop of Woolwich, London

———————

Having parents who divorced when I was a child, I am painfully aware of some of the unhelpful attitudes and teaching, inside and outside the church, which can circulate regarding divorce, remarriage, and singleness. However, I have also experienced how a loving and inclusive Christian community that emulates Jesus' meeting of everyone with a compassionate awareness of the complexities of life and relationships, can bring healing, dignity, and renewal.

I hope and pray that Andy Economides' book will encourage Christian communities to extend Jesus' compassion to everyone, regardless of their relational situation, to enable all to live an abundant and full life in God's loving gaze.

Revd Steve Marsh
The Church of the Good Shepherd
Leighton Buzzard, Bedfordshire

As someone who has experienced the pain of divorce, I can safely say that it is an agonising experience that I would not wish on anybody. But there is healing, hope, and life after divorce because God is always able to rewrite the story of our lives.

I hope that this book from Andy Economides will be a great help to many as they seek to grapple with what the Scriptures say about divorce, remarriage, and being single. Jesus, who is full of grace and truth, will always be the good news for us all, whatever our back story.

Matt Summerfield
Senior Pastor, Zeo Church
Hitchin, Hertfordshire

'He who wears the shoes knows where they pinch.' Revd Andy Economides draws upon his own experience and wisdom and has produced a profound yet simple book. He utilises Scripture, Christian scholars and experts to give us Bible-based truths on the subject of Christian marriage, divorce, and remarriage.

Many African Christians are suffering in silence on these matters as they are confused on what is true Bible teaching on divorce, remarriage, and singleness. Andy Economides' teaching on Malachi 2:16 is an eye-opener. This will help Christian counsellors, teachers, and preachers of God's word in their ministries.

Pastor Bamidele T. Lasisi
New Life For All Nations Ministries, Nigeria

About the Author

Andy Economides is an international speaker and author of eight books. He equips and inspires Christians in effective leadership, in reaching out and caring for the poor and needy. He is an enabler, helping and mentoring pastors and evangelists in their own tasks of ministry.

His work and passion are sharing the Good News of Jesus and bringing people to know and follow Christ. Particular emphasis is given to the maturity of (new) believers and in assisting people to reach their full potential.

Andy Economides is the founder of Soteria Business School (SBS) in Ibadan, Nigeria, West Africa. The school is affiliated to Chichester College, West Sussex, UK. Chichester College Diplomas have been awarded to successful SBS students on completion of the two-year Administration, Computing and Business course. Scholarships for young adults and children are provided through Soteria Trust with the help of sponsors.

Andy originally qualified as an engineer and worked for six years in research and development. For ten years he was on the staff of a church as the lay minister and evangelist. In 1989 St John's Theological College, Nottingham, awarded Andy the College Hood for Theological and Pastoral

Studies. In 1994 Andy became founder and director of Soteria Trust, a registered charity. He ministers under the council of Soteria Trust. Revd Andy Economides OSL is an ordained Christian minister.

If you would like to know more about the ministry of Andy Economides through Soteria Trust, would like to receive the Soteria News, or would like to order any of the resources available, please complete the response slip at the back of this book or visit our website at www. soteriatrust.org.uk.

CONTENTS

INTRODUCTION

Myths Hurt People

Most people believe, and I have heard it said many times, *'No one is indispensable.'* This saying or slogan is a myth. A myth is a widely held but false notion. The apostle Paul, writing to the Christians at Corinth, said the opposite to the words in the slogan. Paul writes:

> *On the contrary, those parts of the body that seem to be weaker are **indispensable.***
>
> 1 Corinthians 12:22

Those Christians in the body of Christ who seem to be weaker are in fact indispensable. Indispensable people are those who are absolutely necessary and vital with an important part to play in the kingdom of God and lives of others.

Many Christians believe, and I have sadly heard it preached and spoken that *'God hates divorce'*. The slogan *'God hates divorce'* is supposed to be based on Malachi 2:16. The slogan is a myth. It is a myth because it is based on an incorrect translation in some Bibles of Malachi 2:16. We shall identify and examine the true translation of Malachi 2:16. We shall also uncover what the Lord is saying in the whole passage (Malachi 2:1-16) about divorce and what was happening in the time of Malachi the prophet.

Truth Brings Life

We know only the truth sets people free. God's word is true. God does not change. Slogans, words and teaching that are myths, untrue or fake, hurt people. Truth matters. Myths damage. Let us speak truth in love. Let us find the truth, believe the truth, teach the truth, and live out the truth by God's grace.

> *If my soul has turned perversely to the dark; if I have left some brother wounded by the way; if I have preferred my aims to Thine; if I have been impatient and would not wait; if I have marred the pattern drawn for my life; if I have cost tears to those I loved; if my heart has murmured against Thy will, O Lord, forgive me.*
>
> *Prayer by F.B. Meyer*

*"The man who hates
and divorces his wife,'
says the Lord,
the God of Israel,
'does violence to the one
he should protect,'
says the Lord Almighty.
So be on your guard,
and do not be unfaithful.*

Malachi 2:16

1. He Hates or God Hates ~ Malachi 2:16

'If he hates and divorces his wife,' says the LORD God of Israel, 'he covers his garment with injustice,' says the LORD of Hosts. Therefore, watch yourselves carefully, and do not act treacherously.

Malachi 2:16 (CSB)

In Malachi's time, the ancient people of God, the Jewish people, the men, were acting treacherously towards the Lord and their wives (Malachi 2:10-16). The men had defiled the Lord's beloved sanctuary and laws by marrying women who worshipped idols. Such marriages between believers and nonbelievers (pagans) were forbidden. Such unions would lead to apostasy. The Lord spoke through the prophet Malachi to the men telling them to guard their hearts and not to deal treacherously towards their wives.

Treacherous Divorce

The men were behaving treacherously, as the New King James Version of the Bible says, and this is mentioned again and again (Malachi 2:10-16). The men hated their wives. This unloving and hurtful behaviour led the men in divorcing their wives. This was treacherous divorce.

'The man who hates and divorces his wife,' says the LORD, the God of Israel, 'does violence to the one he

*should protect,' says the LORD Almighty. So be on your
guard, and do not be unfaithful.*

Malachi 2:16

The men were putting away their wives, divorcing them
and thereby overwhelming the women with cruelty. Their
husbands were covering their own lives with crime and sin.

Who is doing the hating in Malachi 2:16? It is not God.
The text says, *'The man who hates and divorces.'* God did
not say *'I hate divorce'* in Malachi. What the Lord through
Malachi condemned was treacherous divorce. That is, the
men who divorced their wives without righteous reason,
such as adultery, but did so anyway because of hatred and
aversion. Malachi and the Lord are saying nothing about
disciplinary divorce in this passage.

Disciplinary Divorce

Disciplinary divorce could be for adultery, abuse, neglect,
or desertion. Disciplinary divorce is not what Malachi
is talking about and against. There are different forms of
abuse. Abuse could be physical, sexual, financial, emotional,
verbal, or spiritual.

God did not condemn *all* divorce in Malachi, nor did God
say, 'I hate divorce.' We should stop using the phrase or
motto, 'God hates divorce.' It will be biblically accurate to
say, 'God does not hate disciplinary divorce, but does hate
treacherous divorce.' It is a mistranslation to say, 'God hates
divorce.' To use such a slogan when referring to yourself
or others can cut like a knife, as if God hates all divorce. It

is important that we are aware of the correct translation of Malachi and understand the context.

Divorce: Treacherous and Disciplinary

We need to understand the difference between disciplinary divorce which is allowed, and treacherous divorce which Malachi and the Lord were not pleased about. Jesus was, and is, against treacherous divorce. The Bible allows disciplinary divorce. Christianity (often) does not. Victims of divorce or marital abuse can suffer greatly, feel great fear and guilt if they believe that God (and perhaps God's people) hates all divorce. Clarity about the meaning of Malachi is essential for well-being.

The Bible allows disciplinary divorce

There are at least 18 scholars or sources that say 'he hates . . . he covers' is the most faithful way to translate the Hebrew, with 'he' being the divorcing husband in Malachi 2:16. These are some of the translations taken from Barbara Roberts' book, *Not Under Bondage: Biblical Divorce for Abuse, Adultery and Desertion:*

- 1927 (J.M.P. Smith) *'For one who hates and divorces,' says the* LORD *God of Israel, 'covers his clothing with violence,' says the Lord of Hosts.*

- 1986 (Westbrook) *For he has hated, divorced . . . and covered his garment in injustice . . .*

23

- 1997 (Sprinkle) *When he hates so as to divorce, says the LORD God of Israel, then he covers himself with lawlessness.*

- 1998 (Stuart) *If one hates and divorces (Yahweh, Israel's God, said), he covers his clothes with crime (Yahweh of the Armies said).*

- 1999 (Shields) *For one who hates and divorces, says Yahweh, the God of Israel, covers his garment with violence, says almighty Yahweh.*

- 2001 (English Standard Version) *For the man who hates and divorces, says the Lord, covers his garment with violence, says the Lord of hosts.*[1]

Some Bible translations that have 'he hates . . . he divorces' as the man doing the hating and divorcing include the Douay-Rheims 1899 American Edition (DRA), 1599 Geneva Bible (GNV), Holman Christian Standard Bible (HCSB), Jubilee Bible 2000 (JUB), New International Readers Version (NIRV), World English Bible (WEB), and the Wycliffe Bible (WYC).

Truth matters. Myths damage

Who Hates . . . Divorce?

Malachi 2:16 is a 'standard' Bible verse regarding divorce often heard in sermons and teaching. Most believers are probably aware of the traditional King James-style rendering of the first part of Malachi 2:16: 'For the LORD God of Israel says that He hates divorce' (NKJV).

Daniel R. Watson is associate professor of the Old Testament at Midwestern Baptist Theological Seminary, Kansas City, USA. Professor Watson has produced an article called 'Who Hates . . . Divorce? A Text-Critical Examination of Malachi 2:16'. Watson's extensive examination is documented (15 pages) in the *Midwestern Journal of Theology*. His investigation is to find out the truth, whether it is the man or God who does the hating in Malachi 2:16. Professor Watson writes:

> *The Holman Christian Standard Bible (HCSB) has a notably different translation: '"If he hates and divorces his wife," says the LORD God of Israel.' . . .*
>
> *In the HCSB, however, the subject of 'hate' is the man doing the divorcing, and the object of the hate is the wife being divorced. Those not only are different translations, but they are also two different ideas.*
>
> *The purpose of this article is to offer the reader some help in evaluating these translations by examining the primary evidence for the original text of this verse in the Hebrew Old Testament. This will be done by considering the options for the original reading indicated by the ancient textual evidence and their support, followed by a suggestion about which (if any) is mostly likely correct.[2]*

Daniel R. Watson makes it clear he has no personal interest in which reading of the text is correct, nor does he seek to influence readers for or against a particular Bible translation. Watson is only interested in finding out the truth.

The Original Text

Watson carries out his examination by looking into the primary evidence, in the order of importance, for the original text of this verse in Malachi 2:16 in the Hebrew Old Testament using: the **Masoretic Text** (MT), the **Qumran** (Dead Sea Scrolls), the **Septuagint** (LXX), the **Peshitta** (Syriac translation), the **Targums** (Aramaic translations of the Hebrew text), and the **Vulgate** (the 'official' Latin translation of the Western church, done originally by Jerome). The Septuagint is the Greek version of the Hebrew Scriptures.

In Watson's article, he shows the Hebrew verse of Malachi 2:16 as in the Masoretic Text and the Qumran with the corresponding English translation beneath. Watson also shows the real Greek verse of Malachi 2:16 from the Septuagint with the English translation and he does the same for the Targums (Aramaic) and Vulgate (Latin). Let us examine the Hebrew text from the Qumran text below as shown in Watson's article.

Qumran Textual Evidence

The evidence of the Qumran comes from manuscript 4QXII[a]. The suggested date for it is mid- to latter second century BC. The words within brackets are missing from the manuscript and therefore reconstructed. The text reads as follows:

שִׂי[לְבוּ] עַל חָמָס יְכַסּוּ יִשְׂרָאֵל אֶל [יהוה אמר] שַׁלָּח שָׂנֵתָה אִם כִּי
תִבְגָדוּ אֹ[וִל] בְּרוּחֲכֶם וְנִשְׁמַרְתֶּם צְבָאוֹת יהוה אָמַר

'For if you have hated (and) divorced,' [says the LORD]
God of Israel, 'they cover My [garment] with violence,'
says the LORD of Hosts. 'So be careful in your spirit and
do [not] deal treacherously.'[3]

Professor Watson's Conclusions

Watson makes five points in his five pages of conclusions as to the correct and best translation and wording of Malachi 2:16. He provides the readers of his article with information helpful for evaluating the translations in differing English versions of Malachi 2:16. This one verse is famous for its contribution to the church's teaching regarding divorce. Watson writes in his conclusions:

1. *The weight of the evidence seems to agree that, contra traditional translations of the MT, God is not the subject of the verb 'hate', whether in first or third person. The subject is the man doing the divorcing. Qumran points to a second person referent, and that reading is supported by the LXX, the Targum and the Vulgate (the Peshitta, as noted, omits the clause) . . .*

2. *It appears that the two best options are either a reading that largely follows the MT or one that largely*

follows the Qumran text. Here, in the judgment of the present writer, is what the best translation of each reading would be:

MT: 'Because he has hated and divorced,' says the LORD God of Israel, 'violence covers his garment (or he covers his garment with violence),' says the LORD of Hosts.

Qumran: 'But if you hate and divorce,' says the LORD God of Israel, 'then violence will cover (or covers) your garment,' says the LORD of Hosts.[4]

Professor Watson points out that the two translations do not differ greatly so choosing between them is not a significant exegetical-theological matter. The difference between the MT and Qumran lies mostly at the start of each text. The MT text takes it as casual. The Qumran text takes it as conditional.

Watson makes it clear that the MT or the Qumran fits the context of Malachi 2:13-16 well. The MT has the advantage of leaving the consonantal text undisturbed. However, Watson would choose the Qumran reading of Malachi 2:16 over the MT. This is because of its readability, its excellent agreement with the LXX and the flow of thought is a little better.

'But if you hate and divorce,' says the LORD . . . Qumran

Not Under Bondage

It is common to hear a Christian pastor or teacher say, or to read in an article or book, 'God hates divorce.' The slogan is only true if we are describing treacherous divorce. However, the three words are possibly damaging to people who should action disciplinary divorce. The slogan 'God hates divorce' has caused such fear in the lives of Christians that they put up with adultery, abuse, or unacceptable neglect rather than employ disciplinary divorce.

Barbara Roberts has written a helpful book called *Not Under Bondage: Biblical Divorce for Abuse, Adultery and Desertion*. In it she examines: abuse, Jesus' and apostle Paul's teaching, 1 Corinthians 7:10-16, and Malachi 2:16. Roberts answers questions such as: Does the apostle Paul permit divorce for an abused spouse? May I remarry if I have suffered divorce? 'God hates divorce'– slogan or scripture? Isn't adultery the ONLY grounds for divorce? If I am the innocent party, why do I feel guilty? Roberts concludes her book with her closing plea.

God does not hate disciplinary divorce

Closing Plea

If I could make one plea it would be that teachers and speakers evaluate what they plan to say by imagining how a victim of marital abuse would be likely to hear their message. Teachers need to ask themselves: 'How would a victim interpret my teaching? Is there anything in what I plan to say that would further entrap a person who is subordinated in an abusive marriage? Would they feel I have condemned and cut off their hope for freedom?' It takes only 11 words to say, 'God hates treacherous divorce, but he does not hate disciplinary divorce.'[5]

'If he hates and
divorces his wife,'
says the Lord of Israel,
'he covers his garment
with injustice,'
says the Lord of Armies.
Therefore, watch yourselves
carefully, and do not
act treacherously.

Malachi 2:16 (CSB)

2. Divorce and Remarriage

Divorce

Divorce and separation are among the most painful experiences in life. The deep hurt can break your heart and life. Only those who have experienced an unwanted divorce or separation can understand and feel the hurt of it all. However, Christ Jesus can heal broken lives and hearts.

The church should be like a hospital to those who are hurt by separation and divorce. To those who feel that they were responsible for such hurt, the church should be a place of repentance, forgiveness, and healing.

To the divorced, the church must offer hope, acceptance, help and practical love but often there is alienation, misunderstanding and judgment. There is misunderstanding because we have not taken the time to talk with people. There is judgment because of pride, even though we are taught by Christ not to judge (Matthew 7:1-5).

In some societies we see different responses to marriage breakdown ranging from disapproval and judgment at one extreme, or where relationships are treated as temporary and only of value for as long as they feel good at the other end of the spectrum.

You and I and the church must have a different response to marriage breakdown than what society offers. Most Christians do not understand what the Old and New

Testament teach on divorce. That is probably because Christians have not studied the subject thoroughly nor had access to good teaching or books. Sometimes people are not willing to change their views or stubborn beliefs.

Four Reasons for Divorce in the Old Testament

The four grounds for divorce in the Old Testament are valid today. The references to divorce in the Bible refer to men divorcing women; however, these principles can be applied in today's world as much for women divorcing men as men divorcing women. Adultery or unfaithfulness can be a reason for divorce if the man and woman cannot be restored. Even when adultery has occurred divorce is not a necessity because forgiveness can be given and received, and the relationship healed.

> *If a man marries a woman who becomes displeasing to him because he finds something indecent about her, and he writes her a certificate of divorce, gives it to her and sends her from his house . . .*
>
> *Deuteronomy 24:1*

When the Hebrew servants got married to a second wife, which was allowed at that time, they promised to provide for their first wife three things: food, clothing, and conjugal love (marital rights). The husband was forbidden to deprive the wife of all three rights.

> *If he marries another woman, he must not deprive the first one of her food, clothing, and marital rights.*
>
> *Exodus 21:10*

If the husband did not fulfil these three promises or vows, he was showing neglect and abuse and the wife was free to go should she choose to if the situation did not improve.

Most Christians do not understand what the Old and New Testament teach on divorce

The Old Testament had sensible laws about divorce. A husband and wife had to keep his or her four marriage vows: to feed, cloth, share conjugal love and be faithful. The material support was food and clothing. The physical affection was conjugal love. These laws covered abusive situations because physical and emotional abuse is an extreme form of neglecting material support or physical affection.

The victim was the only person who could choose to get a divorce. If your spouse broke their marriage vows, you could choose to divorce them, or you could choose to forgive them and endeavour to save and restore the marriage. A partner could not simply be divorced just because they wanted to, although this had changed by the time of Jesus.

Divorce in Jesus' Time

At the time of Jesus, according to Jewish law a man had the right to divorce his wife. The husband had to simply give the divorce document to the woman in the presence of two witnesses and she was divorced. During that time there were two different schools of thought as for the grounds for divorce based around the interpretation of Deuteronomy 24. This passage allowed divorce when a husband found out 'something indecent' about his wife. The strict school led by Rabbi Shammai, taught that 'something indecent' meant marital unfaithfulness and that was the only allowable cause for divorce.

According to the liberal school led by Rabbi Hillel, a husband could divorce his wife 'for any and every reason'. Rabbi Hillel emphasised the preceding clause, *'who becomes displeasing to him'* (Deuteronomy 24:1) and would allow divorce if the wife did anything the husband disliked. This included the wife gossiping in the street, losing her looks, having an unsightly mole, putting too much salt in his soup, or burning his food while cooking it.

In other words, the wife could be divorced for anything the husband disliked about her. Although ridiculous, this sorry state of affairs existed. These two different schools of thought were vigorously debated among the Jews in Jesus' day.

The wife could be divorced for anything . . . ridiculous

One day the Pharisees came and tested Jesus by asking Him if He agreed to Hillel's liberal view. They wanted to know if it was lawful for a man to divorce his wife for 'any and every reason'.

> *Some Pharisees came to him to test him. They asked, 'Is it lawful for a man to divorce his wife for any and every reason?' 'Haven't you read,' he replied, 'that at the beginning the Creator "made them male and female," and said, "For this reason a man will leave his father and mother and be united to his wife, and the two will become one flesh?" So they are no longer two, but one. Therefore, what God has joined together, let man not separate.' 'Why then,' they asked, 'did Moses command that a man give his wife a certificate of divorce and send her away?' Jesus replied, 'Moses permitted you to divorce your wives because your hearts were hard. But it was not this way from the beginning. I tell you that anyone who divorces his wife, except for marital unfaithfulness, and marries another woman commits adultery.' The disciples said to him, 'If this is the situation between a husband and wife, it is better not to marry.'*
>
> *Matthew 19:3-10*

The first thing we notice from Jesus' teaching is that marriage is designed to be for life. This is God's ideal plan for marriage. Some people believe a husband and wife are joined together in marriage in such a way that they cannot be divided except through death. Jesus taught that, *'Therefore, what God has joined together, let man not separate.'*

The important point is that marriage is permanent, and divorce should be ruled out, not because marriage cannot be broken, but because it ought not to be broken. God's plan is for marriage not to be broken but it can be.

God's plan is for marriage not to be broken but it can be

Jesus' view of marriage was challenged by the Pharisees (who wanted to harm him) when they said to him, *'Why then did Moses command that a man give his wife a certificate of divorce and send her away?'* (Matthew 19:7). Jesus corrected this wrong attitude by telling the Pharisees that the Jewish people were never commanded to divorce their wives, but that divorce was allowed as a concession *'because your hearts were hard'*. Divorce was not compulsory, although it was permissible.

Jesus teaches that divorce is allowed if there has been marital unfaithfulness. In these extreme cases a marriage can be ended. However, an act or more than one act of adultery or marital unfaithfulness does not mean that the other partner has biblical grounds for divorce. Marriages can be restored. Christian couples have to do everything possible to avoid divorce. Many couples have had their marriages saved by working through problems or unfaithfulness or adultery.

Jesus did not believe it was lawful for a man to divorce his wife for *'any and every reason'*. Jesus' answer to the Pharisee's question in Matthew 19:3 was in one word: No.

The Apostle Paul and Divorce

Paul teaches about couples already married and then one of them becomes a Christian. He says they should remain together but if the unbelieving partner leaves and will not return, the believer can with clear conscience let him or her go (1 Corinthians 7:15).

Paul is saying to believers that they can accept abandonment as a valid divorce or reason for divorce. If they were a victim of desertion, they had the right to divorce on the grounds of neglect. Sometimes a partner is no longer a true believer; that is someone who is following the ways of Christ. If such a person leaves their married partner, the marriage can be permanently ended by divorce.

> *But if the unbeliever departs, let him depart; a brother or a sister is not under bondage in such cases.*
>
> *1 Corinthians 7:15 (NKJV)*

Paul is advising and therefore it is not a command from Jesus when he says, *'I, not the Lord'* (1 Corinthians 7:12). However, Paul has wisdom for those who (now) have a non-believer as a spouse that may want to depart, meaning divorce. The Greek New Testament word 'depart' (*chorizo*) means 'to place space between, to separate'. In the first century *'chorizo'* was one of the terms used for legal divorce.

Paul is saying in such circumstances, if an unbeliever departs or separates from the believer, let him or her depart. Paul does not want a believer to be living in a permanent state of bondage and discord. If the unbeliever were 'forced' to live with the believer, there would be no peace in the home. We are called to live in peace and not under bondage.

When looking at 1 Corinthians 7:15 perhaps the most important question to ask is *'Who caused the separation?'* not just *'Who walked out?'* The unbeliever is doing the separating and he or she has destroyed the covenant. Who and what caused the separation are the big issues.

Paul accepted all four Old Testament grounds for divorce. He acknowledged 'unfaithfulness' as a reason for divorce because Christ taught this. Paul accepted the neglect of food, clothing, and conjugal love in Exodus 21:10-11 as grounds for divorce.

Other extreme cases for separation and/or divorce might be if a husband or wife is on the receiving end of physical or mental abuse. In such cases there is no choice but to leave.

Remarriage

In the time of Jesus, it was generally assumed that divorced people would remarry. Permission to remarry for divorced people was understood, acceptable and normal for nearly all cultures in the ancient world. In Jesus' time, divorced women had little option but to remarry because there were no paid jobs for women and no social security.

The church should be like a hospital to those who are hurt by separation and divorce

---

Adultery, Divorce and Remarriage – Exaggerated Teaching

Jesus' words about divorce from Matthew 5:27-32 are often misunderstood today. This continues to cause serious disagreements, problems, judgment and division amongst Christians and churches. To make His point, Jesus often exaggerates, and He is not to be taken literally when He does not intend us to do so. Jesus says:

> *You have heard that it was said, 'Do not commit adultery.' But I tell you that anyone who looks at a woman lustfully has already committed adultery with her in his heart. If your right eye causes you to sin, gouge it out and throw it away. It is better for you to lose one part of your body than for your whole body to be thrown into hell. And if your right hand causes you to sin, cut it off and throw it away. It is better for you to lose one part of your body than for your whole body to go into hell. It has been said, 'Anyone who divorces his wife must give her a certificate of divorce.' But I tell you that anyone who divorces his wife, except for marital unfaithfulness, causes her to become an adulteress, and anyone who marries the divorced woman commits adultery.*
>
> *Matthew 5:27-32*

A few people in the early church took these words of Jesus literally. Democritus did this in the second century and took his eye out. Origen, also in the second century, castrated himself to stop sinning. Jesus is not teaching self-mutilation, for even a blind man can lust. By exaggeration Jesus is making his point: that is, be drastic about wrong ways, attitudes, and sin. Jesus is not saying that lust was literally adultery any more than a person should tear their eye out. Jesus is not saying that those who remarry are literally committing adultery.

Remarriage by a divorced person is not adultery. Jesus was referring to people who used the Mosaic certificate of divorce, where there was no unfaithfulness, to justify abandoning a marriage partner and marrying someone else. Jesus regarded this divorcing as wrong and 'invalid'. Jesus is saying that remarriage after 'invalid divorce' is not right and this new marriage is no different to 'committing adultery'.

Jesus is not saying that those who remarry are literally committing adultery

---

Remarriage should not be taken for granted even when divorce ends a marriage legally and morally. After divorce, people have the freedom to remarry but some people may make a prayerful decision not to. This is a matter in which to seek the Lord, pray for the Lord's guidance and will as to remarry or stay single. People should not remarry in order to solve their problems.

Divorced people need to get sorted out first anyway. Taking baggage into another relationship would not be helpful. It is vital to take time to heal from the hurt and brokenness. Lessons can be learned. We can rebuild carefully and prayerfully. We need wise and faithful friends and counsel to point us towards Christ and His ways. We all must be careful not to make hasty judgments about divorced people or single people for that matter.

My Story of Hope

There is life after separation and divorce. The ongoing pain and hurt of a distressing marriage are truly devastating. Suffering such hurt is crushing and it affects your mental and physical well-being. Separation and divorce are like a bereavement. It brings deep grief to lose someone you love, with whom you have a vision and purpose for yourselves, others, and Jesus.

It is at times like these that you need friends. Friends that will stand by you and help you in the way you need. I have needed such friends with wisdom, understanding, and love as I have faced my own deep loss, separation, divorce, and pain. I have tried to support others who faced the most painful and distressing separation and divorce.

We can comfort those in any trouble with the comfort we ourselves receive from God.

2 Corinthians 1:4

Who helped me through this hurtful time? Firstly, the Lord Himself gave me His love, peace, and restoration. The healing continues. Several Christians provided wisdom, understanding, clarity, compassion, and support. I received at least three words of knowledge and prophetic words from those who knew nothing of my situation. I held on to those words tightly with God's own word and presence.

Counsellors

A Christian counsellor assisted me to understand the situation and enabled me to have courage to move forward.

A relationship needs boundaries to be healthy and spiritually alive. Repeated destructive behaviour in a relationship from one person towards the other harms the friendship. Progress can only be achieved if the destructive person sees and owns up to the hurt they are causing. For counsellors trying to assist in such matters much wisdom is needed. For counsellors to act neutral in the matter only enables the person's self-deception to grow unchallenged. Sin hidden harms, but honesty means restoration (Proverbs 28:13).

It is not appropriate for counsellors or pastors to take a neutral position when having a face-to-face meeting with the perpetrator and victim. The effect of neutrality can be devastating.

Neutrality is not neutral. Neutrality effectively means you become an ally of the abuser, because by taking the view that both parties are contributing to a marriage problem, then you are effectively saying, 'It is not abuse.' This only serves the agender of the abuser.

'Recovery from Divorce and Separation' is a seven-part course and is helpful in bringing healing. It is suitable for Christians and non-Christians. Those who have been separated or divorced for a short or long time find the course worthwhile. The course has come out of Holy Trinity Brompton, London. It is available in the UK in different towns and cities.

Mistreatment of Divorced People

I have heard wrong teaching and seen behaviour that has led to the mistreatment of divorced people. Dr George Verwer DD, founder of Operation Mobilisation, in his book *Confessions of A Toxic Perfectionist and God's Antidote*, writes:

> *I have learned so much from people and families that have gone through difficult times, some of them going through divorce. With over 200,000 former OMers, we have a lot of opportunities to learn from the trials and experiences of dear friends. I have continued to be in touch with a few thousand, and more and more of them are in heaven.*

> *Something in me, I believe put there by Jesus, reaches out to those who have suffered, including the loss of loved ones, especially children, financial failure, divorce, or worse. It has led me to a more realistic understanding of life on our fallen, rebellious planet.*

I have had an extra special interest in couples who met on OM, but those marriages broke. Well over a thousand couples have met on OM, especially on our four different ships. OM actually pioneered in accepting divorced people coming into global missions. We now have a long history of outstanding divorced people being used of God. I believe it is wrong teaching and toxic perfectionism that led to the persecution and mistreatment of divorced people for a couple of thousand years.[6]

Forgiveness

Forgiveness is absolutely necessary. How can we know when there is no forgiveness? You know when there is no forgiveness, when revenge is given out because someone feels hurt or sinned against. Revenge may be an action or the opposite, the silent treatment. Revenge from not forgiving destroys relationships. Jesus Christ taught us to forgive those who sin against us (Luke 11:4).

Total forgiveness is not taking revenge. This daily forgiveness Christ demands is necessary to restore broken communion with God. If we do not forgive others the sin against us, our heavenly Father will not forgive us. But if we do forgive others, our Father will forgive our sins (Matthew 6:14-15). The word of promise of Christ has a condition. From the cross, Jesus cried out, *'Father, forgive them, for they do not know what they are doing'* (Luke 23:34). During this difficult time, I have been called upon to forgive others by not taking revenge.

Total forgiveness is not taking revenge

The book *Divorce and Remarriage in the Church*, by Dr David Instone-Brewer, helps us to understand what the Bible teaches on this subject. He is Senior Research Fellow in Rabbinics and New Testament, Tyndale House, Cambridge, UK (www.instone-brewer.com). He is not divorced or separated and no one in his family has been. For anyone who is divorced or separated or wants to get remarried in church it will prove to be most pastoral.

I thought I had some understanding of divorce and remarriage until I read this book. I discovered what the Bible says about divorce. It is an excellent book, and I cannot recommend it highly enough. All church leaders should read it. It will help them to look after those in their care.

3. SINGLESNESS

To be single means you are one. Being single as a Christian is different, or should be, from being single in our society. Society does not follow the teaching of Christ. In society or Christian culture singles are a diverse group and can include:

- Single, never married, with no sexual experience.

- Single, with a history of cohabitating or other sexual relationships.

- Single, never married, with a child or children – a lone parent.

- Single but previously married, now separated, divorced, or widowed with or without children.

Some single people live alone, others with a family, others with friends, and others with parents or children. Voluntary singleness is where people are single by choice or calling. Involuntary singleness is where people are single by circumstances or social reasons.

Single Myths

Singleness is not a punishment or second best. Marriage is not a higher calling than being single. Not all singles are discontent or dissatisfied. Singles are not necessarily more self-centred than married people. Singles are not necessarily more sexually frustrated than married people.

Singleness is not an indication of immaturity, deep emotional problems, or something wrong. Singles are not necessarily preoccupied with finding a spouse. Singles do not necessarily have more free time than married people. Singles are not necessarily lonelier than married people.

Some Truths

Married people can be very sexually frustrated. There can be more loneliness in marriage than single people experience. Single people can be busier than married people.

As followers of Christ, some people are called to be single, others to be married. Some people should get married, others stay single. We are not all the same. God gives some the gift of marriage, and to others He gives the gift of singleness (1 Corinthians 7:7). Singleness should be promoted positively as an equal option and should never automatically be interpreted as a lonely existence or a relational vacuum.

Singleness and Generosity

The challenge for all people, whether single or married, is to be a generous person with the time, talents, and treasures that our Lord has given us. A single person's life should not revolve around themselves. A single person's motto should not be, *'It's all about me.'* Jesus, a single person, said: *'I did not come to be served but to serve'* (Mark 10:45).

Jesus' life on earth was one of great generosity. Christ served others instead of expecting others, or waiting for others, to serve Him. Jesus washed His friends' feet, cooked their breakfast, and went without food in order to care for others.

> *Apart from sexual temptation the greatest danger, which I think we face, is self-centredness. We may live alone and have total freedom to plan our own schedule, with nobody else to modify it or give us advice. If we are not careful, we may find the whole world revolving around ourselves.*
>
> *Revd John Stott*

I did not come to be served but to serve

Jesus did not regard His own life as His own, doing exactly what He wanted just because He was single. His time, energy, finances, and focus were spent towards others. Being a single man, I should not always expect others to invite me to their home for a meal. It is a blessing when that happens. I often initiate having meals with others in a restaurant or café.

Solitude, Community and Church

Single people need solitude. It is also necessary for single people to be part of community. Single people must be included in the makeup of what we describe as community and church. Single people are as much part of the church as married people, *but it does not always feel like that.*

You can be at peace, happy, and blessed on your own. We are human beings not human doings. Single people do not always have to be busy doing something. Life is made up of work, rest, and play.

> *Loneliness is inner emptiness. Solitude is inner fulfilment. If we possess inward solitude, we do not fear being alone, for we know that we are not alone.*
>
> *Richard Foster*

You can be at peace, happy, and blessed on your own

People were created with a two-fold need: fellowship with God and companionship with other human beings. Fellowship with God is the solution for loneliness. Companionship with fellow Christians is the cure for aloneness.

Oswald Sanders

Honesty

It is better to be honest than to pretend and wear a mask. We can be honest with God about how we feel with our struggles as a single person. We need to be more open and honest with people. We can show grace by allowing those around us to be honest about the challenges they face in their situations.

We can give permission to others to ask us tough questions. Others can ask for our help and we shall not make them feel guilty or judge them. Mary, a Christian, says:

I am single now but was married for 14 years. I miss the sex and love we enjoyed when married. It is not easy to live without that as a single person today. People do not understand. They do not ask about that.

Relinquishment and Singleness

To relinquish means to give up something. Discipleship as a single person means freedom as I relinquish. We can confess if having a boyfriend or girlfriend or spouse has become an idol. The idol can be relinquished. We can let go or relinquish our loss or dreams that have not been realised and we can give ourselves time to grieve to help us do that.

We can trust God that He knows what is best for us and that He can see the bigger picture even when we cannot. We can respect and value each individual person we meet as a person made in the image of God and not to immediately judge them on their potential to be a partner.

Family Defined by Jesus

One day Jesus was talking to the crowd and His mother and brothers stood outside wanting to speak to Him. Someone interrupted Jesus to say that His mother and brothers were standing about and wanted Him. Jesus answered the person:

'Who is my mother, and who are my brothers?' Pointing to his disciples, he said: 'Here are my mother and brothers.' For whoever does the will of my Father in heaven is my brother and sister and mother.'

Matthew 12:48-50

Jesus cut the emotional and physical ties

Jesus' family expected Him to just stop what He was doing and attend to them and their request. Family ties are very strong but sometimes most unhelpful or unhealthy. Jesus did not elevate His mother and brothers above others and above the will of God. It was necessary for Jesus to continue to do the will of God which was to teach the crowd.

Jesus' mother and brothers had to learn that Jesus could not just be pushed around or ordered about. Jesus also had His own boundaries, and He did not let His family cross them. Jesus cut the emotional and physical ties that were no longer needed. Jesus redefined the meaning and purpose of family. Jesus now taught that the people who do the will of God are His family. The disciples and crowd were His family. For singles, our family is everyone who does the will of God. This is family.

Contentment

The world is not content. We are being challenged every day to acquire more and get something better or newer or bigger. *'Godliness with contentment is great gain'* (1 Timothy 6:6). The grass is greener where you water it. But we often think the grass is greener next door. Single people should cultivate a heart of contentment. A relaxed attitude lengthens life. Put it another way, *'A heart at peace gives life to the body'* (Proverbs 14:30).

Single people do not need to be jealous or feel envy of married people or those in relationships. It would help if we set our vision on Jesus to allow our perspectives to be set by God's values rather than the world's values. Single people can live in the present without the need to be waiting for a better day. This is the day that the Lord has made, let us rejoice and be glad in it. Your life is not on hold. Rejoice.

Single and Life to the Full

> *We must counter the social lie that sexual intercourse is necessary for fulfilment in life. Jesus teaches us that it is perfectly possible to be single, celibate, and human at the same time.*
>
> *Revd John Stott*

Jesus was single. He never married and He lived life to the full. This Jesus promises us fullness of life today (John 10:10). How did Jesus live His life? Firstly, He spent *time* with His heavenly Father on His own. Jesus called out to others to go with Him and be with Him. He invested in *friendship* (Mark 3:13). Jesus had many friends not just a few. He spread Himself around. That is healthy. He did not put all His eggs in one basket. Jesus asked His closest friends for *support* at times (Matthew 26:38).

My closest friends have given me their support in difficult and painful times, and it has made all the difference. *Jesus shared meals with people* (John 21:12). This is important for single people to do. Jesus was not afraid of physical *touch* as a single man. We do not have to be prudish or afraid to touch. Jesus knew His boundaries and kept them.

Jesus allowed Himself to be anointed and touched by a woman who had a sinful past. She knelt at His feet weeping at a dinner party. Her tears fell on His feet and she wiped them with her long, beautiful hair. Then she kept kissing His feet and putting perfume on them (Luke 7:36-50). Living a single life does not eliminate you from deep levels of human interaction, heart exchange, and touch.

> *Single adults are more intimacy starved than sexually deprived.*
>
> *Elaine Storkey*

Testimony by Jill

Jill is an exceptional and highly talented professional teacher and lecturer. Jill has been part of the UK Soteria Trust teams visiting Nigeria, teaching, and speaking. She says:

> *Reflecting back, much of my 20s was spent wondering when I was going to meet a life partner. Scouring through my old journals I seemed to have given quite a lot of*

emotional time and energy in asking God to fulfil this desire for me and relieve me from the single life.

In my early 30s this was still the case in part, however I had moved into a new phase of my life having made changes to leave my job and go on to further study in mission and ministry.

At this point the college I attended was full of single people in their 20s and 30s and it was refreshing and life changing to be in an environment where the majority of people were single and focused on what God had called them to be – namely disciples of Jesus Christ and to go on and make disciples of all nations.

There is no hierarchy of status in God's family

I gained a huge amount by being surrounded by those who were not worried by their single status and saw it as a great opportunity to serve God and be available to Him. This excited me as it was out of the box in terms of what I had previously experienced and encountered with other singles who had struggled.

It helped me to lift my eyes to God's horizon and know that there was so much more to life than the marriage and family option. There was God's world to explore, His kingdom plans to be a part of and His wider family to get to know!

It was at this time I was truly able to cultivate and develop my relationship with God and focus much more on the new possibilities that were out there for me to serve Him.

Having left my job I no longer defined myself by what I did, which was teaching. I was actually beginning to understand my identity in God, and that first and foremost I was His child, accepted and loved. I realised there is no hierarchy of status in God's family.

Whether single or married we are precious to God and one is not better than the other. Yet we have all been shaped and influenced by our culture and for the most part been led to believe that being married is a better option than being single.

That message has been also communicated in the church despite the fact that our two great heroes of the faith, Jesus and Paul, were both single and both lived lives of incredible richness and fulfilment.

Peace and Contentment

Jill's testimony continues:

During my mid-30s I did get engaged but as the time moved closer to marriage it became clearer to me that this was not the path that I was to go down. It was a complex time of trying to discern what I thought God was saying and discover what I truly wanted for the life God had given me.

I had no peace in moving forward and experienced a radical redirection in my life. It was an 'Emmaus road' experience for me in the sense that my journey was interrupted; Jesus met with me and redirected me on to a new path.

I did not reach the destination I was headed for; in the same way the two disciples did not reach Jerusalem. Everything I thought I wanted was right in front of me and yet I could not move. The Lord searched my heart in a deep and profound way.

Single or married . . . one is not better than the other

It was very painful, and the journey beyond this decision has not been easy. Yet God has given me an abundance of peace and contentment for the place I am in and I am so grateful for that. I have been able to embrace the many good things about the single life.

God has blessed me with new purpose and meaning in my life; the riches of loyal and meaningful friendships; the expansion of my gifts of skills; time to travel; the chance to explore new creative projects; the enjoyment of mixing with amazing godly people from a whole variety of backgrounds and experiences, and the completion of some life-long goals.

I have realised that so much time and emotional energy can be spent in looking for fulfilment in that one true relationship rather than looking to God. If only we embrace God and what He has for us each day, then we can know true contentment and fulfilment in our lives. Each day is a gift from Him, and we can rejoice and be glad in it.

So, if you are single and are reading this, I hope it encourages you to look up and out to the things of God and know that you can experience complete love and acceptance from Him; nurture your friendship with God.

If you are married please continue to bless your single friends with the gift of friendship, you both need it. If you are a church leader please value and respect the single people you have in your congregation – there are probably more singles now than ever before attending your church. Please acknowledge them just as much as the married couples and affirm them in their gifts and calling.

ENDNOTES

[1] Barbara Roberts, *Not Under Bondage: Biblical Divorce for Abuse, Adultery and Desertion* (Maschil Press, 2008), pp. 127, 129.

[2] Daniel R. Watson, 'Who Hates . . . Divorce? A Text-Critical Examination of Malachi 2:16' (*Midwestern Journal of Theology* 10.1, 2011), pp. 87-102.

[3] Daniel R. Watson, 'Who Hates . . . Divorce?' p. 92.

[4] Daniel R. Watson, 'Who Hates . . . Divorce?' pp. 98-99.

[5] Barbara Roberts, *Not Under Bondage*, p. 113.

[6] George Verwer DD, *Confessions of A Toxic Perfectionist and God's Antidote* (Good Shepherd Books, 2020), pp. 46-47.

א יצק כבוד ש
שב לא תוצא בצרוס להא
רית הוא ושחד בצולם היא צ טבא פ
ל אלוא התוספי כהא עצה ציא כידא
ינו לורבוס כאי המאמג וכרות שאון
נו ישיא מש יעשה תצוני וסתר ה
להיות כמו שיא מלהתקדש עם
יו אל כאשף שרת לורצו ה

Further Information about SOTERIA TRUST

Sponsorship Changes Lives

Soteria Trust is a registered charity based in Emsworth, Hampshire, with Revd Andy Economides the founding director. Soteria Trust helps vulnerable young people (aged 16 plus) including those who have no parents, those who are extremely poor, or women who could be sexually exploited. Young people are awarded scholarships to study at the Soteria Business School in Ibadan, Nigeria, West Africa. Soteria Trust also provides sponsorship for Soteria School staff.

Children (aged 4–18 years) who are poor or needy are also awarded sponsorships to attend Prospect School in Ibadan – a combined primary and secondary school which Revd Andy Economides helped to build by raising funds to purchase the land.

You can make a difference by sponsoring a young person, child, or staff worker for £19 per month. You can sponsor more than one if you wish. Please ask for a pack for your kind consideration. Email us on admin@ soteriatrust.org.uk, telephone on 01243 377315 or return the slip below.

- -

Please send me a sponsorship pack for

❏ Child   ❏ Young Person   ❏ Soteria School Staff

❏ I don't mind who I sponsor (apply to greatest need)

My name (BLOCK CAPITALS):

....

My address: ....

....

.... Post code: ....

My phone no: ....

My email: ....

Please return this slip to:
Soteria Trust, 39 North Street, Emsworth, Hampshire, PO10 7DA, UK

Sponsorship Changes Lives

My name is Ola★: I was given a scholarship at
SBS by Revd Andy to study Administration,
Business and Computing and later awarded
a scholarship to study ATS – Accounting
Technician Scheme. I was able to proceed
to polytechnic for HND with my AAT
certificate and undergo the National Youth Service Corps.
I worked a few years since 2014 with my International
Diploma certificate from Chichester College and later was
able to set up my own Creative Digital Agency here in
Ibadan. We design websites. The course at Soteria Business
School has been so helpful and I can say I am a better
person today. God bless Revd Andy and my sponsor.

My name is Francis★: I came to the Soteria
Business School and was awarded a scholarship
with feeding and accommodation. I was also
fed with the word of God all through my stay.
After my two-year course in Administration,
Business and IT at SBS I was able to get a
job with the diploma given to me by the school to work
as an IT Administrator. With this job, I was able to feed
myself and help my family. I have an admission to study
nursing in a nursing college in Ogun State Nigeria. I am
grateful to God and Soteria Trust for the great privilege as
my ambition is finally coming to pass.

★ Names have been changed.

SOTERIA BUSINESS SCHOOL
Ibadan, Nigeria, West Africa

Soteria Business School (SBS) is an Innovation Enterprise Institution approved by the Ministry of Education of Nigeria. SBS is affiliated to Chichester College in the United Kingdom. SBS provides training and awards national diplomas. The professional courses include:

- NID Business Informatics
- NID Software Engineering
- NID Hardware Engineering
- Accounting Technician Scheme (ATS)
- Data Processing
- Software and Hardware Engineering
- Website Design
- Microsoft Applications and Desktop Publishing

Soteria Business School provides excellent teaching and hostel facilities with affordable fees. The school has a well-equipped library and computer rooms. SBS has a solar system which supplies regular and better electricity.

The Vision of Soteria Business School

- Education for Jobs
- Values: Excellence, Honesty, Compassion and Determination
- Teaching Christ in Word and Action

For more information:

You are welcome to visit. Register for full-time or part-time courses from 3 months to 2 years. The Soteria Business School has courses Monday to Friday and Saturday for specific professional studies. Come and see for yourself.

Soteria Business School, Beside DB Petrol Station, Bola-Ige Bus Stop, Liberty Road, Oke-Ado, Ibadan, Nigeria.

Tel: +234 (0)703 0049999, +234 (0)802 7685159

Email: soteriabusinessschool@gmail.com

Website: www.soteriaschool.com

Resources Available

TRUE

If you are a Christian this book will refresh your soul by showing you Jesus Christ again. If you have never seen Jesus Christ clearly, in these pages you will see him standing before you. And when our tired, unseeing eyes are opened to glimpse him, he is indeed the most beautiful sight for sore eyes.

From the foreword by J.John.

Sale price: £5 Normally: £6.99

TRUE RELATIONSHIPS

Blessing others; forgiving others; loving others; love, sex and marriage; the greatest friendship – mentoring; the impacting friendships of leaders; relationships to avoid; recovering from spiritual abuse; divorce and remarriage; trust; singleness; friendship with Christ.

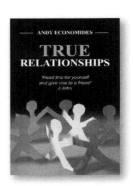

Sale price: £5 Normally: £8.99

REFRESHED AND RENEWED

Provides a weekly word for daily living for the whole year with 53 short chapters. Refreshed and Renewed looks at the life of Jesus Christ and His transforming power today by taking us through the gospel of John for 21 weeks. This is Andy Economides' first weekly word for daily living (hardback with ribbon).

Sale price: £10 Normally: £12

RESTORED & REVIVED (Hardback)

Restored & Revived provides a weekly word for daily living for the whole year with 52 short chapters. It explores the work of the Holy Spirit through the life of the early believers by looking at Acts for 29 weeks. Restored and Revived also looks into important relationship areas including boundaries, confrontation, and letting go. This is Andy Economides' second weekly word for daily living (hardback with ribbon).

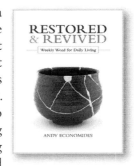

Sale price: £12 Normally: £15

RESTORED & REVIVED (Softback)

Restored & Revived provides a weekly word for daily living for the whole year with 52 short chapters. It explores the work of the Holy Spirit through the life of the early believers by looking at Acts for 29 weeks. Restored and Revived also looks into important relationship areas including boundaries, confrontation, and letting go. This is Andy Economides' second weekly word for daily living (softback).

Sale price: £10 Normally: £12

These books are available from the Soteria Office and can also be ordered by completing the slip opposite and sending to:

Soteria Trust, 39 North Street, Emsworth, Hampshire, PO10 7DA, UK

My Response Slip

My information request

❏ I would like to receive Soteria News regularly.

My regular giving

❏ Send me information on how I can give regularly to Soteria Trust.

My one-off gift

❏ I enclose a gift of £ .... for Soteria Trust.

Cheques should be made payable to SOTERIA TRUST and sent with slip.

My order	Cost	P&P	Quantity	Total
True	£5	free		
True Relationships	£5	free		
Refreshed & Renewed	£10	free		
Restored & Revived (hardback)	£12	free		
Restored & Revived (softback)	£10	free		
He Hates or God Hates	£7	free		
			TOTAL	

My name (BLOCK CAPITALS):

....

My address: ....

....

.... Post code: ....

My phone no: ....

My email: ....